MYSTERIES OF SPACE

INVESTIGATE!

ARE BLACK HOLES REAL?

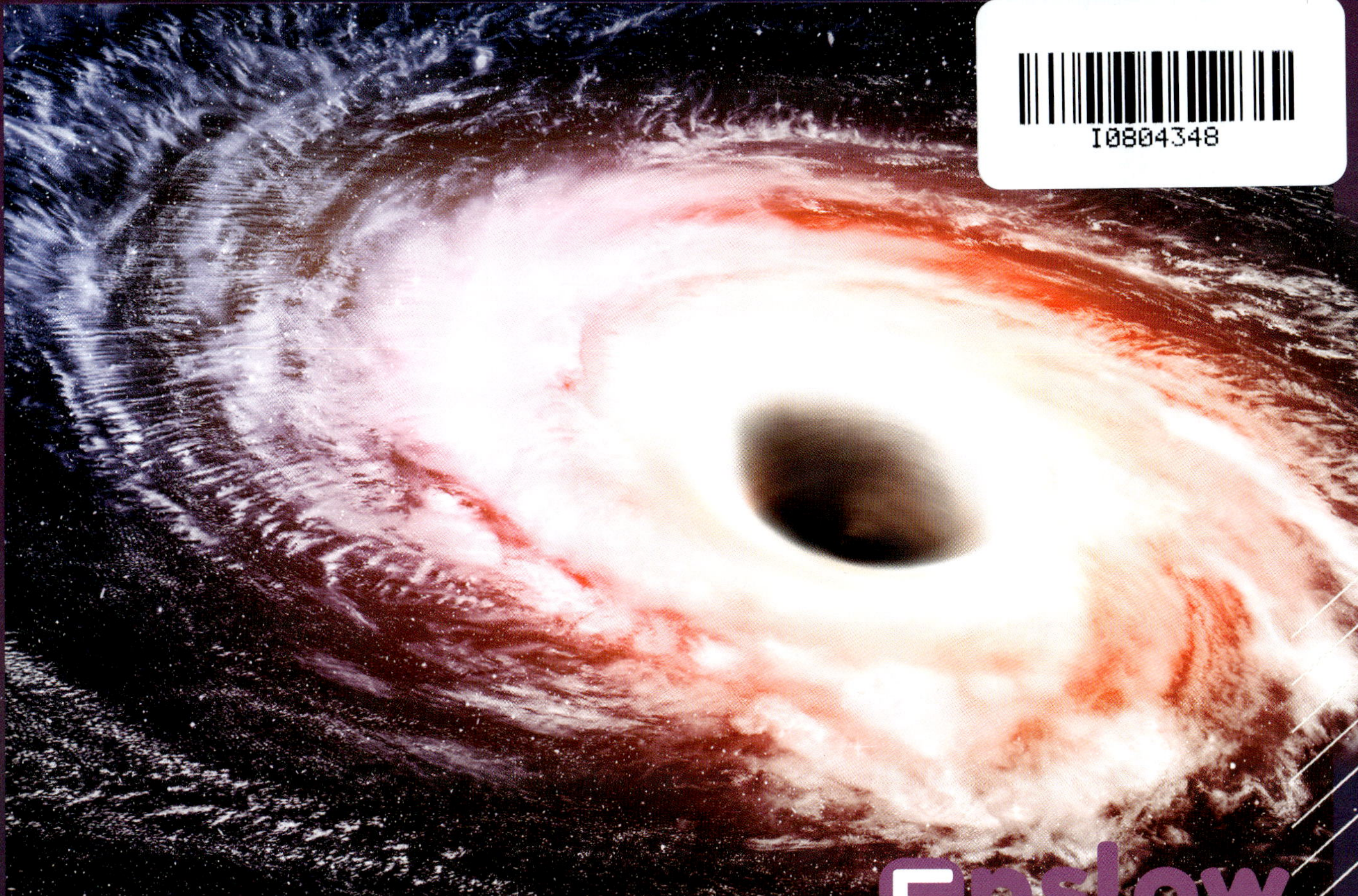

BY SOPHIE WASHBURNE

Enslow PUBLISHING

Please visit our website, www.enslow.com.
For a free color catalog of all our high-quality books, call toll free 1-800-398-2504 or fax 1-877-980-4454.

Cataloging-in-Publication Data

Names: Washburne, Sophie.
Title: Are black holes real? / Sophie Washburne.
Description: New York : Enslow Publishing, 2024. | Series: Mysteries of space | Includes glossary and index.
Identifiers: ISBN 9781978535275 (pbk.) | ISBN 9781978535282 (library bound) | ISBN 9781978535299 (ebook)
Subjects: LCSH: Black holes (Astronomy)--Juvenile literature.
Classification: LCC QB843.B55 W37 2024 | DDC 523.8'875--dc23

Portions of this work were originally authored by Greg Roza and published under the title *What Is a Black Hole?* All new material this edition authored by Sophie Washburne.

Published in 2024 by
Enslow Publishing
2544 Clinton Street
Buffalo, NY 14224

Designer: Tanya Dellaccio Keeney
Editor: Jennifer Lombardo

Photo credits: Cover (logo) AAVAA/Shutterstock.com; series background Molibdenis/Shutterstock.com; cover REDPIXEL.PL/Shutterstock.com; p. 4 muratart/Shutterstock.com; p. 5 Anna L. e Marina Durante/Shutterstock.com; pp. 7, 9, 25 courtesy of NASA; p. 8 https://upload.wikimedia.org/wikipedia/commons/2/2b/Eagle_Nebula_from_ESO.jpg; p. 11 VectorMine/Shutterstock.com; p. 13 https://upload.wikimedia.org/wikipedia/commons/c/cf/Black_hole_-_Messier_87.jpg; p. 15 (sun) Claudio Caridi/Shutterstock.com; p. 17 PatinyaS/Shutterstock.com; p. 19 (*Interstellar*) Kathy Hutchins/Shutterstock.com; p. 19 NASA images/Shutterstock.com; p. 21 kovalto1/Shutterstock.com; p. 23 IvaFoto/Shutterstock.com; p. 26 IgorZh/Shutterstock.com; p. 27 Vadim Sadovski/Shutterstock.com; p. 29 Alones/Shutterstock.com.

Printed in the United States of America

CPSIA compliance information: Batch #CSENS24: For further information contact Enslow Publishing at 1-800-398-2504.

CONTENTS

Words in the glossary appear in **bold** type the first time they are used in the text.

THE GRAVITY OF THE SITUATION

Gravity is an invisible, or unseen, force that pulls things toward each other. This force pulls rocks and dust together to form planets, keeps our planet **orbiting** the sun, allows the moon to create tides, and makes things fall when you drop them.

The more mass something has, the higher its gravitational force is. This means it's harder for things to get away from it. For example, the sun is the largest thing in our **solar system**, so all the planets orbit around it instead of flying off into space.

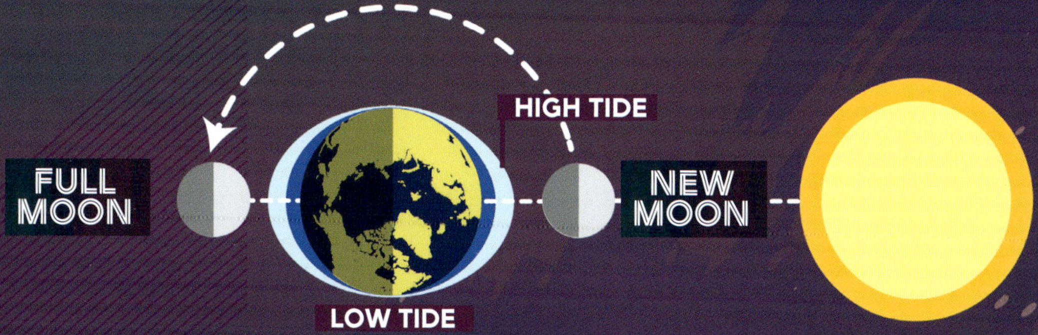

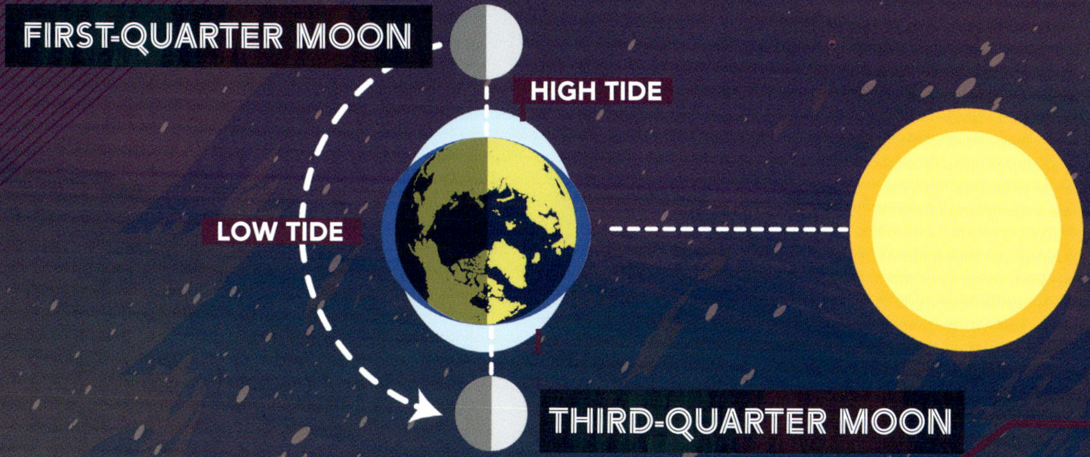

THE MOON'S GRAVITY PULLS ON EARTH'S OCEANS, CREATING LONG WAVES CALLED TIDES.

EXPLORE MORE!

IT TAKES BOTH LIGHT AND GRAVITY EIGHT MINUTES TO TRAVEL FROM OUR SUN TO EARTH. THIS MEANS THAT IF SOMETHING WERE TO HAPPEN TO THE SUN, WE WOULD SEE IT AND FEEL IT EIGHT MINUTES AFTER IT HAPPENED.

NO ESCAPE

A black hole is an object in space that's so massive, or giant, nothing—not even light—can escape its pull! Anything that gets close to a black hole is pulled into it due to its strong gravity.

Because black holes pull in light, they're invisible. Scientists can find them by watching what the stars around them do. If the stars are orbiting something invisible, scientists can tell there might be a black hole there. Then they can use special tools to take a closer look.

SCIENTISTS BELIEVE THERE'S A BLACK HOLE AT THE CENTER OF EVERY LARGE **GALAXY**. THIS PHOTO SHOWS THE CENTER OF OUR GALAXY, THE MILKY WAY.

EXPLORE MORE!

BLACK HOLES DON'T GIVE OFF LIGHT. HOWEVER, THEIR GRAVITY MAKES THE OBJECTS NEAR THEM GIVE OFF A SPECIAL KIND OF LIGHT WE CAN'T SEE WITH OUR EYES. SCIENTISTS USE TOOLS TO SEE AND MEASURE THIS LIGHT TO HELP THEM FIND BLACK HOLES.

A STAR IS BORN

In every galaxy, there's a lot of swirling gas and dust moving around. If enough of this gas and dust piles up in one place, gravity pulls it into a clump called a nebula. As this nebula grows larger and more massive, its gravity increases and pulls in even more matter. Parts of the nebula spin and grow **denser**, becoming stars.

When matter gets denser, it also gets hotter. A star's core, or center, is very hot and dense. This heat gives off light, which is how we can see stars from Earth.

EXPLORE MORE!

THE PLURAL OF NEBULA IS "NEBULAE." THERE ARE MORE THAN 20,000 NEBULAE IN OUR GALAXY ALONE, AND THERE ARE BILLIONS OF GALAXIES IN THE **UNIVERSE**!

THIS PHOTO SHOWS A CLOUD OF DUST IN THE EAGLE NEBULA.

A star's core powers it for millions, billions, or even trillions of years. After that time, it uses up all of its fuel and dies. This means it can no longer continue to give off heat and light. Gravity pulls much of the star's matter into its core, making it even denser.

Stars come in different sizes. When small ones die, they become brighter and then their light burns out. Much more massive stars, however, end life in a huge, bright explosion called a supernova. After that, some stars turn into black holes.

EXPLORE MORE!

A STAR THAT ISN'T QUITE BIG ENOUGH TO BECOME A BLACK HOLE BECOMES A NEUTRON STAR WHEN IT DIES. A NEUTRON STAR IS A VERY SMALL BUT DENSE STAR.

STAR LIFE CYCLE

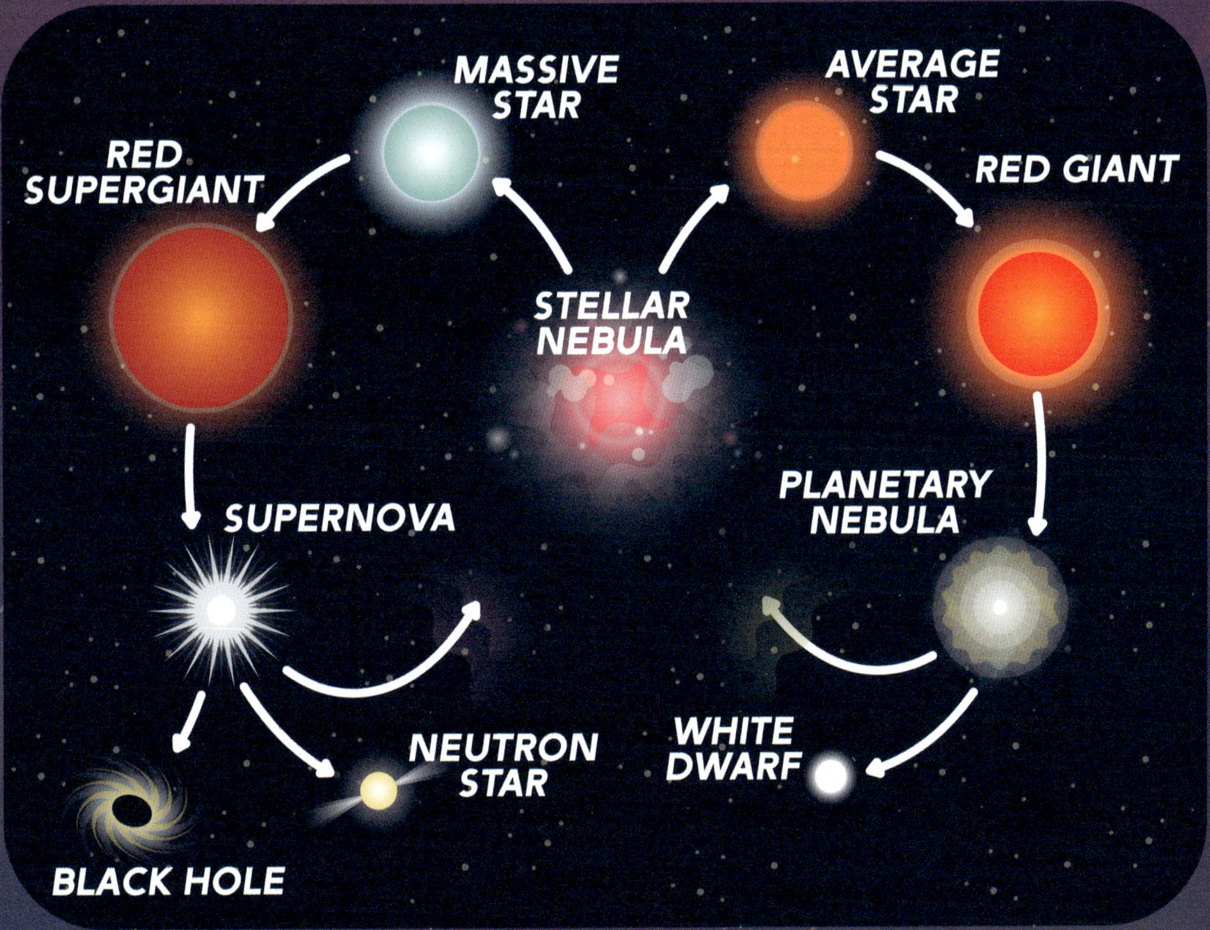

ONLY CERTAIN KINDS OF STARS BECOME BLACK HOLES, AND ONLY UNDER CERTAIN CONDITIONS.

BECOMING A BLACK HOLE

After a supernova, the core of some dying stars grows smaller. However, this core continues to pull in matter as it shrinks, becoming denser and more massive. The gravity created by the shrinking core becomes huge, pulling in everything around it.

This means that while a black hole looks like empty space, it's really filled with an incredible amount of matter packed into a very small space. If the star has about two to three times the mass of our sun in its final stage, it has so much gravity that it must become a black hole.

THIS BLURRY PICTURE IS THE FIRST PHOTO OF A BLACK HOLE, TAKEN IN 2019. AS PEOPLE MAKE **TELESCOPES** MORE POWERFUL OVER TIME, WE MAY SEE MUCH CLEARER PHOTOS.

EXPLORE MORE!

MASS AND VOLUME ARE TWO DIFFERENT THINGS. MASS IS HOW MUCH "STUFF" IS IN SOMETHING. VOLUME IS HOW MUCH SPACE IT TAKES UP. A BLACK HOLE HAS A LARGE MASS AND A SMALL VOLUME.

TYPES OF BLACK HOLES

Black holes come in different sizes. The smallest ones may be as small as a single **atom** but have as much mass in them as a mountain. Scientists believe they may have formed when the universe was created.

The largest black holes are called "supermassive." They have more mass inside them than 1 million suns. The supermassive black hole at the center of the Milky Way galaxy has as much mass as 4 million suns and as much volume as a few million Earths.

EXPLORE MORE!

THE MOST COMMON KIND OF BLACK HOLE IS CALLED A STELLAR BLACK HOLE. "STELLAR" MEANS STAR. STELLAR BLACK HOLES ARE SMALLER THAN SUPERMASSIVE BLACK HOLES, BUT THEY'RE STILL VERY LARGE.

IMAGINE A STAR 10 TIMES MORE MASSIVE THAN OUR SUN SQUEEZED INTO AN AREA THE SIZE OF NEW YORK CITY. THAT'S HOW DENSE A BLACK HOLE IS.

GETTING CLOSE

It's possible to orbit a black hole without getting pulled into it. In fact, many black holes have a ring of matter orbiting them. This matter is called an **accretion** disk.

The closer you get to a black hole, the greater the pull of its gravity becomes. Finally, you'd reach an area called the event horizon. An event horizon is a point in space near a black hole where the gravity becomes too strong to escape. An object would have to move faster than the speed of light to get away!

THIS PICTURE SHOWS WHAT SCIENTISTS BELIEVE A BLACK HOLE LOOKS LIKE UP CLOSE. THE LIGHT AROUND IT IS THE ACCRETION DISK.

EXPLORE MORE!

THE EVENT HORIZON GETS ITS NAME BECAUSE IT'S THE BORDER, OR HORIZON, PAST WHICH WE CAN'T SEE ANY EVENTS THAT ARE HAPPENING INSIDE THE BLACK HOLE.

PULLED IN!

According to the laws of **physics**, once an object crosses the event horizon, it won't stop falling toward the center of the black hole, where the gravity is strongest.

The center of a black hole is called the singularity. It's a point where the density is infinite, or endless, but the volume is zero. That means a limitless amount of matter fits in a space that doesn't exist. How can this be? In reality, the singularity can't possibly exist. Scientists just don't know what's actually there.

EXPLORE MORE!

WHEN SCIENTISTS TALK ABOUT THE SINGULARITY, THEY'RE TALKING ABOUT THE WAYS OUR KNOWLEDGE FALLS SHORT. THE MATH AND SCIENCE THEY'VE DONE SO FAR AREN'T ENOUGH TO TELL THEM WHAT REALLY HAPPENS IN A BLACK HOLE.

THE 2014 MOVIE *INTERSTELLAR* IMAGINED WHAT MIGHT HAPPEN TO SOMEONE WHO FALLS INTO A BLACK HOLE.

WHAT'S INSIDE?

Scientists have a lot of theories, or ideas, about what happens inside a black hole. Right now, we don't know for sure if any of them are true. One theory is that every black hole has what's called a "white hole" on the other side.

Many scientists don't believe white holes exist because, unlike black holes, we've never found any. Scientists who believe in them say a white hole would look just like a black hole, but it would spit out the things the black hole on the other side pulls in.

THE CONNECTION BETWEEN A BLACK HOLE AND A WHITE HOLE WOULD BE CALLED A "WORMHOLE." THIS PICTURE SHOWS WHAT A WORMHOLE MIGHT LOOK LIKE.

EXPLORE MORE!

IF WHITE HOLES DO EXIST, THEY'RE THE OPPOSITE OF BLACK HOLES. JUST AS NOTHING CAN ESCAPE A BLACK HOLE PAST ITS EVENT HORIZON, NOTHING WOULD BE ABLE TO ENTER A WHITE HOLE.

Though we're learning more about them all the time, black holes are one of the great mysteries of the universe. Some scientists as well as science-fiction writers believe that black holes have wormholes that lead to other locations in the universe—or even a totally different universe.

Many scientists believe our universe started from a singularity. That could mean we're inside a black hole right now, and every black hole has another universe inside it. This is just a theory some scientists have. They can't prove that it's true.

EXPLORE MORE!

SPACE AND TIME ARE CONNECTED. IF WORMHOLES ARE REAL, THEY COULD LEAD FROM ONE POINT IN SPACE TO ANOTHER, ONE POINT IN TIME TO ANOTHER, OR A COMBINATION OF BOTH.

THIS PICTURE SHOWS THE IDEA THAT THERE ARE OTHER UNIVERSES INSIDE OUR OWN. HOWEVER, EVEN IF THIS WERE POSSIBLE, IT'S UNLIKELY THE GATEWAY BETWEEN THEM WOULD LOOK LIKE THIS.

SPAT OUT

While it's true that black holes pull in matter and grow denser, many also emit, or spit out, matter that hasn't passed through the event horizon. Supermassive black holes emit high-speed, very hot jets of a type of matter called **plasma** from their centers. In 2021, scientists proved that this is caused by a **magnetic field** within the accretion disk.

Some black holes emit so much radiation, or waves of energy, they grow less massive and their gravitational force decreases. However, this happens so slowly that it doesn't make much of a difference in how the black hole acts.

WE CAN'T TAKE A PICTURE OF A BLACK HOLE EMITTING A PLASMA JET LIKE THIS, BUT THIS PICTURE SHOWS HOW SOME PEOPLE IMAGINE IT WOULD LOOK.

EXPLORE MORE!

SCIENTISTS KNOW BLACK HOLES EMIT PLASMA JETS BECAUSE THE JETS ARE VERY HOT. WITH SPECIAL TOOLS THAT LET THEM SEE HEAT AS ENERGY WAVES, THE SCIENTISTS CAN FIND THE JETS.

ARE WE SAFE?

To many people, black holes are scary! They want to know if they could get sucked into one and what would happen if they did. The bad news is that if a person fell into a black hole, they would die. The good news is that it's impossible for anyone living on Earth to do that!

There is a supermassive black hole at the center of the Milky Way, but it isn't sucking the Milky Way into itself. Also, our sun isn't a big enough star to ever become a black hole.

BLACK HOLES DON'T USUALLY TRAVEL AROUND SPACE, SO IT'S LIKELY IMPOSSIBLE FOR ONE TO APPEAR WITHOUT WARNING NEXT TO OUR PLANET.

EXPLORE MORE!

EVEN IF OUR SUN COULD BECOME A BLACK HOLE, IT WOULDN'T SUCK OUR SOLAR SYSTEM INTO IT. THE BLACK HOLE WOULD HAVE THE SAME GRAVITY AS THE SUN, SO EVERYTHING WOULD KEEP ORBITING IT.

MORE TO LEARN

Scientists have already learned so much about black holes, but there's still a lot they don't know. They're very interested in learning more because black holes might be able to tell them about how galaxies form. For example, do black holes help galaxies form, or do they form at the same time?

Knowing more about this might even be able to help scientists figure out how the universe started. This knowledge could answer many other questions we have about space, our planet, and ourselves.

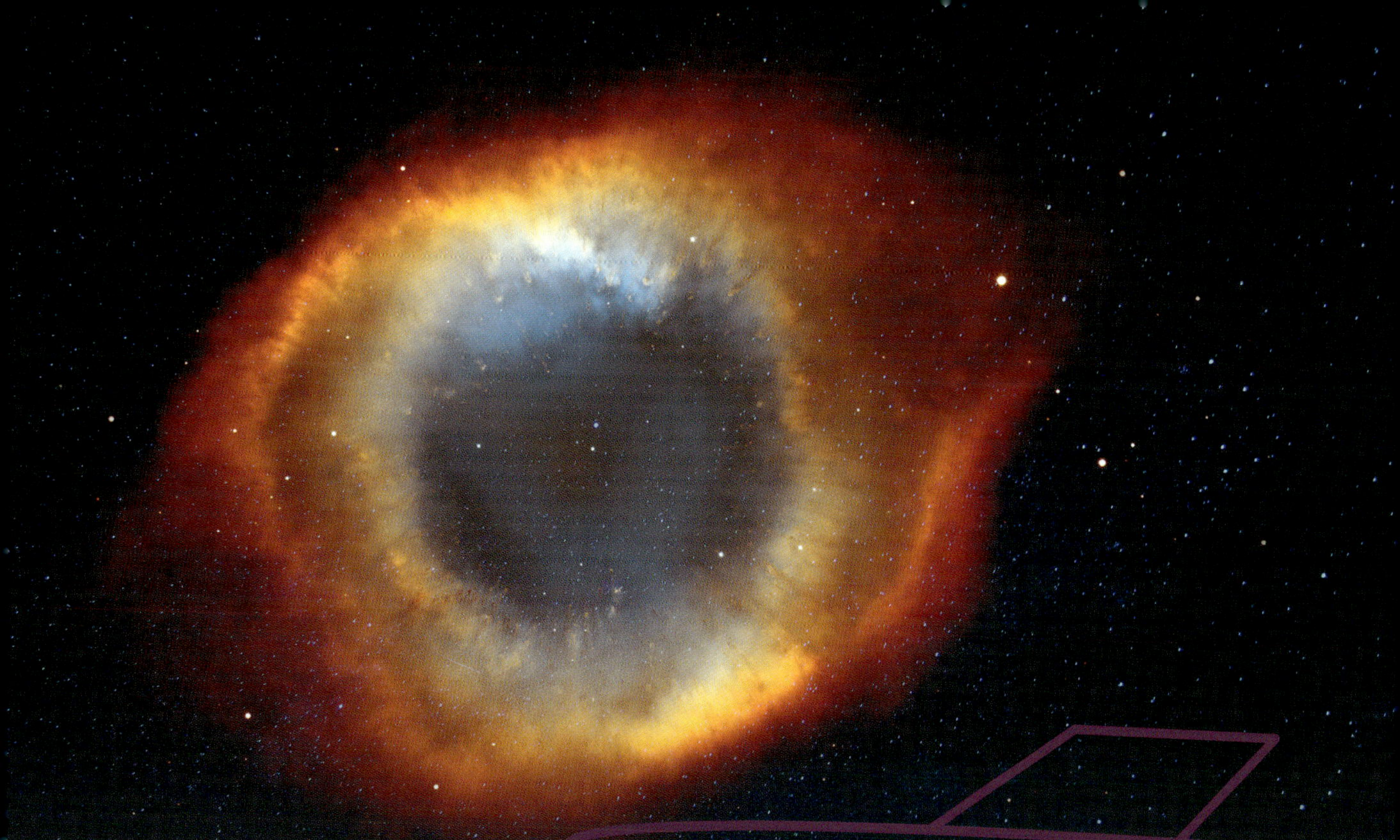

THE BEST EXPLANATION WE HAVE FOR THE START OF THE UNIVERSE IS THAT IT EXPLODED FROM A SINGULARITY. STUDYING BLACK HOLES MIGHT HELP SCIENTISTS FIGURE OUT WHERE THAT MATTER CAME FROM.

EXPLORE MORE!

AFTER THE UNIVERSE FIRST EXPLODED, IT EXPANDED, OR GREW OUTWARD, VERY QUICKLY. WITH SPECIAL TOOLS, SCIENTISTS HAVE PROVEN THAT IT'S STILL EXPANDING MORE SLOWLY TODAY.

GLOSSARY

accretion: A building up of matter over time.

atom: One of the smallest bits of matter.

dense: Having matter in a given area that is close together.

galaxy: A large group of stars, planets, gas, and dust that forms a unit within the universe.

magnetic field: The area around a magnet or magnetic body where its pull is felt.

orbit: To travel in a circle or oval around something, or the path used to make that trip.

physics: The study of matter, energy, force, and motion, and the relationships among them.

plasma: A collection of charged particles that shows some characteristics of a gas but that differs from a gas in being a good conductor of electricity.

solar system: The sun and all the space objects that orbit it, including the planets and their moons.

telescope: A tool that makes faraway objects look bigger and closer.

universe: Everything that exists.

FOR MORE INFORMATION

BOOKS

Erlic, Lily. *Black Holes.* New York, NY: AV2, 2020.

Green, Joel. *Black Holes.* Chicago, IL: Norwood House Press, 2023.

Loh-Hagan, Virginia. *Black Holes.* Ann Arbor, MI: Cherry Lake Publishing, 2021.

WEBSITES

BrainPOP: Black Holes

www.brainpop.com/science/space/blackholes

Watch a movie and take a quiz to test your black hole knowledge.

Ducksters: Black Holes

www.ducksters.com/science/black_hole.php

Read more cool facts about black holes.

Planets for Kids: Black Holes

www.planetsforkids.org/galaxies/black-holes.html

Learn more about what black holes are and how they form.

INDEX